Ribbon Stash Mini-Book

Can't remember the ribbons you have? Organize your collection with this fun book.

SIZE: 4" x 5"

MATERIALS:

Black Stiffened Eazy Felt • Felt (Pink, Purple, Blue, Hot Pink) • 2 binder rings • Ribbons • 4 Clear rhinestones • Decorative paper • Cardstock • Chipboard letters • Chipboard • Crop-A-Dile • Corner rounder • Sewing machine • Thread • Cuttlebug die cut machine with flower dies • Adhesive

INSTRUCTIONS:

1. Cut 2 pieces of stiffened felt, 2 decorative papers, and 2 pieces of chipboard 4" x 5".
2. With sewing machine, Zigzag stitch around each felt.
3. Die cut felt flowers for the front and back covers.
4. Adhere flowers to the front and back cover as desired. Add rhinestones in the center of each.
5. Adhere title as desired
6. Adhere decorative papers to inside of each cover.
7. Cut cardstock $3\frac{7}{8}$" x $4\frac{7}{8}$". Round outer corners.
8. Cut 2 holes into each cardstock and cover.
9. Add binder rings; decorate the rings with ribbons.

Pencil Holder + Pen Cover

by Rocio Duran

Perfect for pens and pencils. This box is easily assembled with tied ribbons.

SIZE: 1" x 10" including ribbon

MATERIALS:

Black Stiffened Eazy Felt • Felt (Pink, Purple, Blue, Lime, Hot Pink) • 12" Pink ribbon • Green embroidery floss • Clear rhinestones • Eyelets • Crop-A-Dile • Sewing machine • Thread • Cuttlebug die cut machine, Flower dies • Adhesive

INSTRUCTIONS FOR BOX:

1. Cut Black pieces: Four $3\frac{1}{2}$" x $4\frac{3}{4}$" for sides, one $3\frac{1}{2}$" x $3\frac{1}{2}$" for bottom.
2. Die cut several felt flowers.
3. Using floss, stitch flower stems. Sew flowers to the top of stems.
4. Punch holes $\frac{3}{4}$" apart along the sides and bottom pieces.
5. Set an eyelet in each hole.
6. Lace the sides together. Lace the sides to the bottom with ribbon.

INSTRUCTIONS FOR PEN:

1. Fold stiffened felt to cover pen. Trim excess felt.
2. Add a piece of ribbon inside the felt.
3. Zigzag stitch around the felt.
4. Die cut 5 different flowers in 3 different sizes. Punch a hole in the center of each flower. Thread ribbon through the hole and tie a knot.

'Us Gals' Felt Mini-book

by Nichole Pereira

Make a mini album that you can carry with you and share with friends.

SIZE: 4" x 4"

MATERIALS:

Felt (6 colors) • Cardstock • Fabric • Decorative papers • Stickers • Chipboard stickers • Binder ring • Ribbon • Photo corners • Sewing machine • Thread • Fabric glue

INSTRUCTIONS:

1. **Book**: Cut 6 squares of cardstock 4" x 4" for the base of your album.
2. Cut 1 felt square of each color 3¾" x 3¾".
3. Create a paper tab for each page and glue in place.
4. Stitch each felt to a cardstock square. If desired, sew a square of fabric to some of the pages.
5. Cut 5 photos 2" x 2", glue to pages. Decorate as desired.
6. **Cover**: Adhere chipboard letters.
7. Punch a hole in the upper left-hand corner, add binder ring and ribbons.

'A Blooming Girl' Scrapbook Page

Felt flowers blooms with dimension and color on a beautiful memory page.

SIZE: 8½" x 11"

MATERIALS:

Felt (Olive Gren, Red, Pink, Yellow, Fuschia) • Tan 8½" x 11" cardstock • Photo corners • Buttons • Letter stickers • Pink embroidery floss

INSTRUCTIONS:

1. Cut out a tree shape from felt and sew it to the page.
2. Cut out felt flowers and Yellow centers.
3. Sew buttons and flowers to cardstock with embroidery floss.
4. Add photos, photo corners and page title.

'Peas in a Pod' Page

Stitch a fabulous textured background for a scrapbook.

SIZE: 8½" x 11"

MATERIALS:
Felt (Blue, Chartreuse) • Fabric • Tan 8½" x 11" cardstock • Rhinestone brads • Chipboard letters • Sewing machine • Thread

INSTRUCTIONS:
1. Cut felt 5½" x 10½" and fabric 3" x 10½". Sew to cardstock.
2. Sew the photo to the page.
3. Add title, felt circles and rhinestone brads.

'She' Page

Felt circles and brads fill the empty spaces on a layout with pattern and color.

SIZE: 8½" x 11"

MATERIALS:
Felt (Ivory, Red, Pink, White, Hot Pink, Brown) • Brown 8½" x 11" cardstock • Paper (White, Pink) • Brads • Chipboard circle • Puffy Paint • Scallop edge scissors • Sewing machine • Thread • Fabric glue

INSTRUCTIONS:
1. Cut 5 felt circles in different sizes from each color.
2. Glue circles to the cardstock.
3. Stitch vertical and horizontal lines over the circles.
4. Add photos, brads, and puffy paint.
5. Cut a scallop corner from Pink and White paper for photo corners. Adhere to top and bottom photos.

See instructions and patterns for stitched flowers on pages 10 - 11.

Growth Chart

by Rocio Duran

Innovative scrapbook techniques embellish a beautiful wall hanging - perfect for a girl's room.

SIZE: 10" x 53"

MATERIALS:
3 sheets 10" x 18" Pink Stiffened Eazy Felt • Ribbons • Flowers • Rub-ons • Rhinestone words • Clear rhinestones • Decorative paper • Chipboard letters • Hat pins • Corner punch • Circle cutter) • Crop-A-Dile • Eyelets • Eyelet tools • Sewing Machine • Thread • Matura MT Script Capitals font • Adhesive

INSTRUCTIONS:
1. Zigzag stitch 2 long sides of the stiffened felt.
2. At the top of one sheet, fold 1" to the back and sew. Thread a 36" ribbon through the pocket and tie in a bow for the hanger. Punch 2 holes in bottom of sheet.
3. Punch 2 holes on the top and bottom of the middle sheet, and 2 holes in the top of the bottom sheet. Set eyelets in each hole.
4. Tie ribbons to connect felt sheets into 1 long one.
5. Decorate as desired. Use hat pins as markings for each time the child is measured.

My Room Door Hanger

by Suzy West

Unless you are going to clean it, knock before entering. Create a fun door hanger for every bedroom in your home.

SIZE: 3½" x 9"

MATERIALS:
Wood door hanger • Felt (Blue, Hot Pink, Stiffened Yellow) • Felt letters • Chipboard letters • Buttons • Cardstock • Black pen • Adhesive

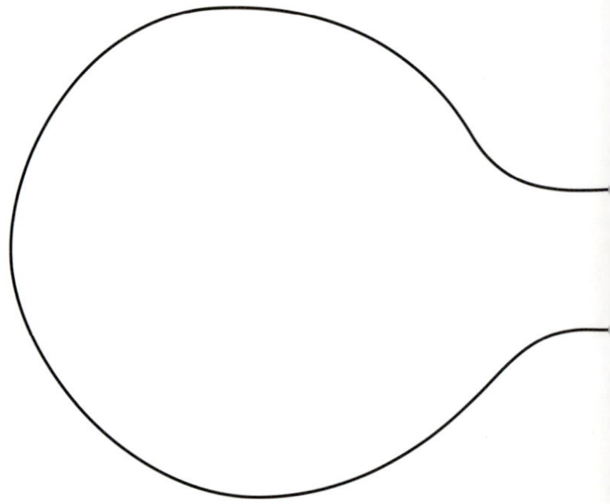

'My Room' Door Hanger Pattern

INSTRUCTIONS:
1. Trace the door hanger onto cardstock.
2. Decorate cardstock with felt letters and flower pieces.
3. Adhere them onto the door hanger.
4. Add felt and chipboard letters.
5. Outline the door hanger with a Black pen.

Live Laugh Love Hanging Sign

by Krista Lund

Keep your priorities in focus with this cute wall hanging.

SIZE: 6" x 12"

MATERIALS:
6" x 12" canvas • 2 screw eyes • Felt (Pink, Purple, Fuschia) • Decorative papers • Cardstock (Pink, Purple) • Ribbon • Die cuts (flower, circle, letters) • Buttons • Font: Pharmacy • Adhesive

INSTRUCTIONS:
1. Cut papers 4" x 6". Adhere to the canvas.
2. Die cut 3 flowers and circles in coordinating colors of felt.
3. Layer flower, circle and button. Sew button to flower. Adhere to canvas.
4. Cut out the title and adhere to the canvas. Embellish with buttons.
5. Attach screw eyes and thread ribbon to create a hanger.

Bib and Booties

Sweet, soft, and simple, this ensemble makes a lovely gift for a baby shower.

SIZE: Newborn

MATERIALS:
Newborn bib and booties • Felt (Pink, Purple, Fuschia) • Die cuts (flower and circle) • 12" Green ribbon • Buttons • Sewing machine

INSTRUCTIONS:
1. **Bib**: Die cut felt flower and circle. Zigzag stitch to the bib.
2. Free-hand cut the letter "k" and adhere to the center of the flower.
3. Zigzag stitch a Green flower stem.
4. Tie a knot in a piece of ribbon and stitch it to the bib forming leaves of the flower.
5. Tie another piece of ribbon around the bib.
6. **Booties**: Die cut 2 felt flowers and circles.
7. Adhere to the booties by stitching on buttons.

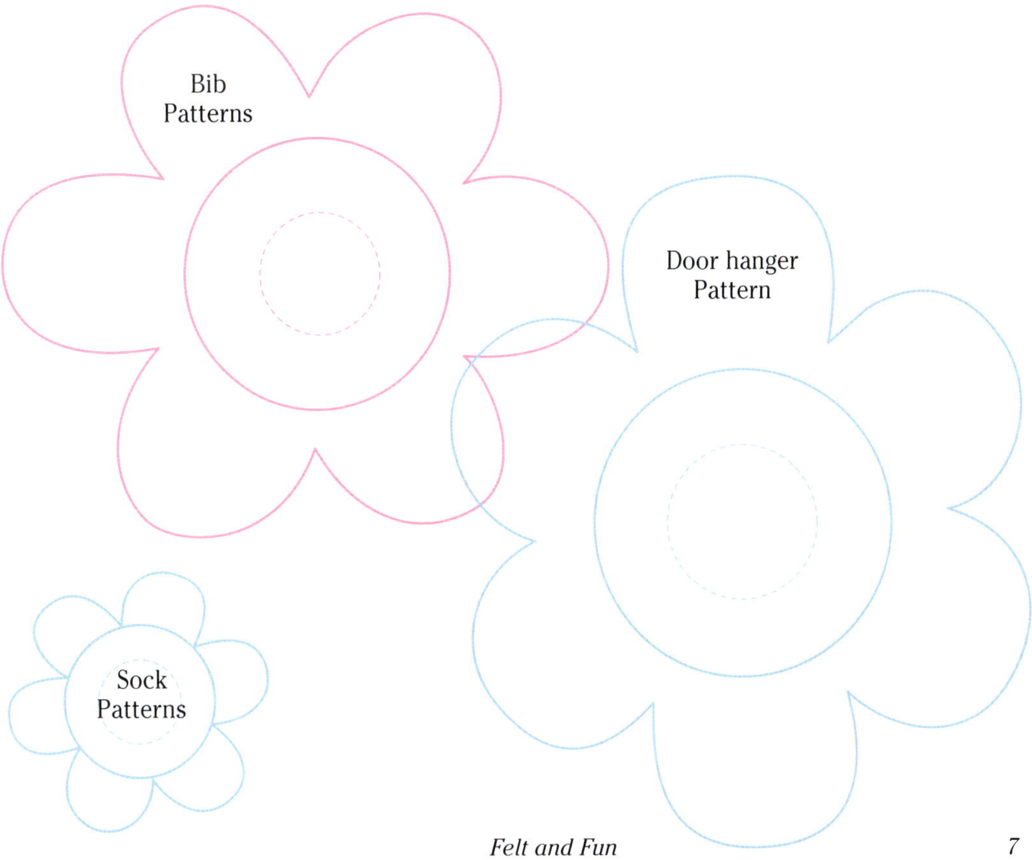

Pirate Birthday Book

by Sylvia Pantoja-Bargas

Ahoy Matey! Tis a birthday we be celebratin' on the high seas. Create an adventurous scrapbook that complements the theme of your party.

SIZE: 6" x 6"

MATERIALS:
Felt (Black, White) • Red rickrack • Cardboard • Cardstock (Black, Red) • Rhinestones • 2 binder rings • Ribbons • Rub-ons • Felt glue

INSTRUCTIONS:
1. Cut the following 6" x 6" pages: 4 Black felt, 3 Red cardstock, 3 Black cardstock, 2 cardboard.
2. Punch 2 holes on the left side of each page for binding. Staple ribbon tabs to pages.
3. Cover cardboard with Black felt.
4. Trace skull and crossbones on felt. Cut out, adhere to cover.
5. Add Red rickrack and rhinestones.
6. Combine all pages and add rings.
7. Add ribbon to rings.

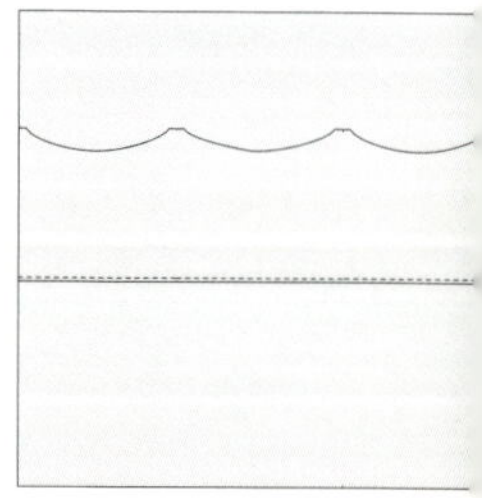

Homework Center

by Rocio Duran

Nifty storage pockets keep your child's room and desk organized.

SIZE: 18" x 23"

MATERIALS:
4 sheets 12" x 18" Black Stiffened Felt • Felt (Green, Navy, Gold, Tan, Burgundy) • *Provo* wood clipboard • Wood letters • White floss • Buttons • Ribbons • Binder rings • Bookplates & brads • Eyelets • Decorative paper • Die cut alphabet • Crop-A-Dile • Black acrylic paint • Paintbrush • Sewing machine • Thread • Adhesive

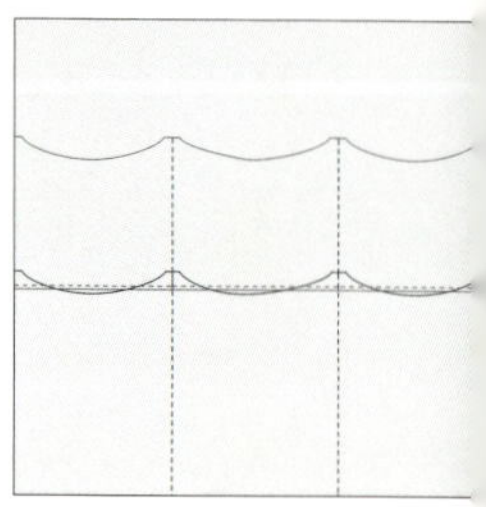

INSTRUCTIONS:
1. Paint clipboard and letters. Let dry.
2. **Background felt**: Sew 2 felt pieces together across the longest side. Cut to 18".
3. **Pockets**: Cut felt to desired length. Add bookplates and buttons. Sew to background.
4. Zigzag stitch around edges. Decorate.
5. Add 2 holes and eyelets to the bottom of the pockets. Add binder rings and clips to each hole. Add ribbon as desired.
6. **Finish**: Decorate wood letters and clipboard.
7. Adhere wood letters to the top of the clipboard with Glossy Accents. Let dry.

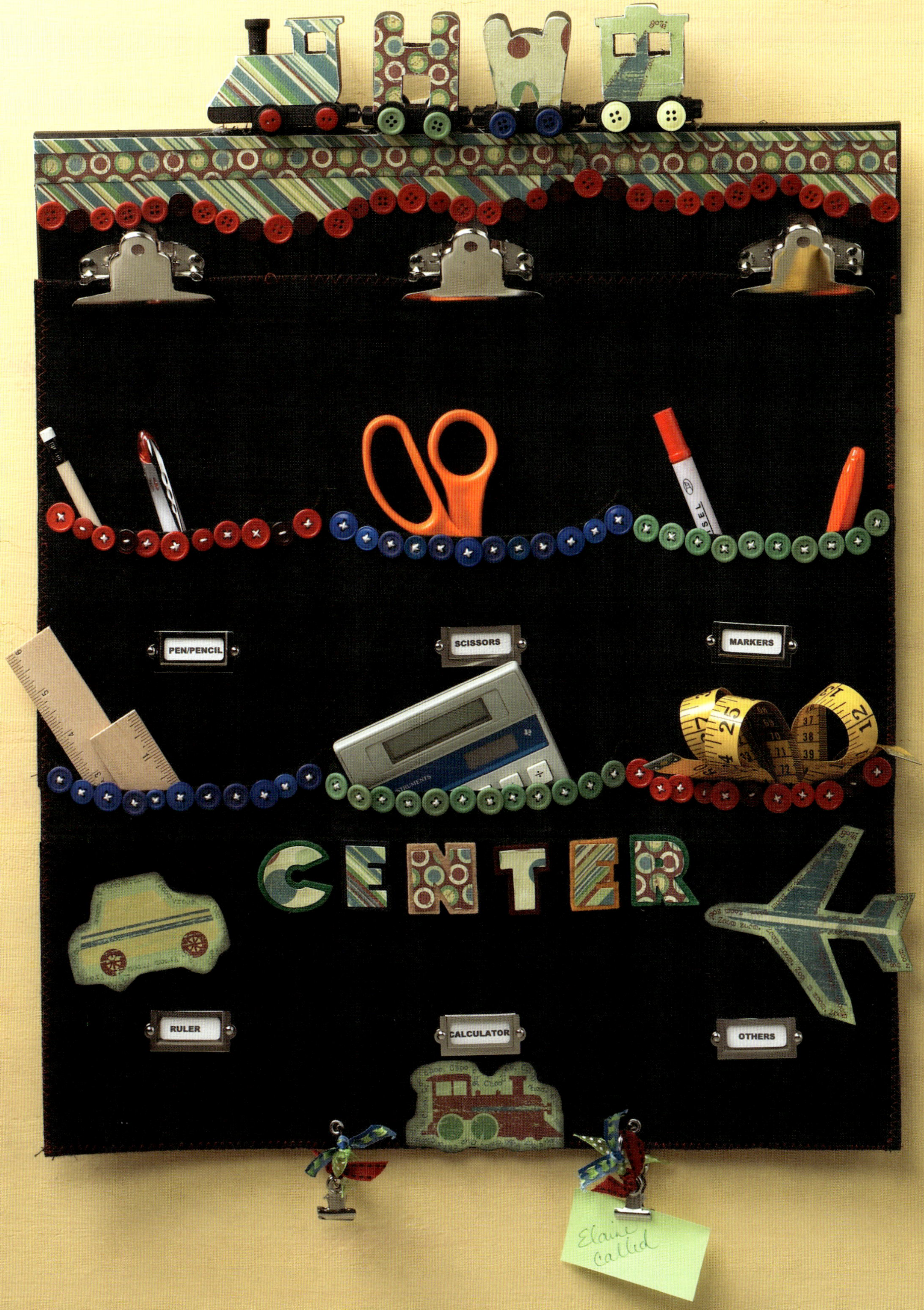
PEN/PENCIL
SCISSORS
MARKERS
CENTER
RULER
CALCULATOR
OTHERS
Elaine called

Flower Magnets

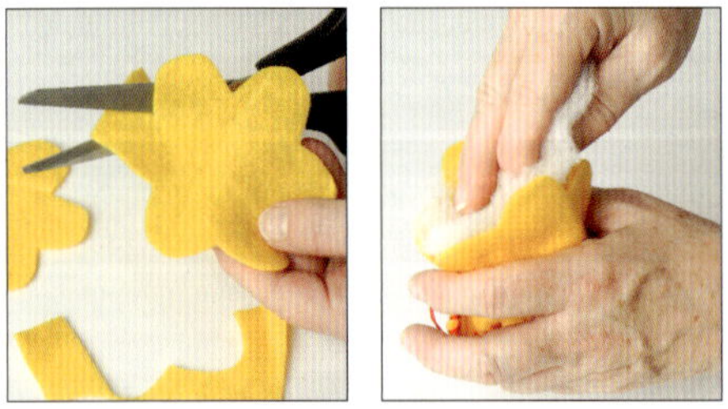

1. Cut out two felt flowers.
2. Layer two felt pieces together. Add polyfil stuffing to the center to make the flower puffy.

3. Whipstitch around the edges with floss or pearl cotton.
4. Join layers by sewing a felt shape and button in the center.

Message Board . . .

by Suzy West

Your family will be drawn like magnets to this eye-catching board. Create a garden of flower magnets for your family board or refrigerator.

SIZE: 18" x 24"

MATERIALS:
Red Stiffened Felt • Lime Green felt • Ribbon • White board • Buttons • White floss • Magnets • Cardstock • *Provo Craft* Cricut • Adhesive

INSTRUCTION:
1. **White board**: Measure a board. Sew strips of felt to fit around the border of bulletin board.
2. Scallop the edges on one side of the felt.
3. Adhere to the board,
4. **Letters**: Die cut letters. Trace die cuts onto felt. Cut out and adhere felt on top of letters.
5. Adhere letters and buttons to board.
6. **Flowers**: Cut felt flowers: 4 large, 2 small.
7. For each flower top, sew 1 small flower to 1 large one with a button.
8. Stack a flower top with a plain back. Leaving a small opening for stuffing, stitch the flowers together. Stuff. Finish stitching.
9. Adhere a magnet to the back of each flower.

Our Shining Star Scrapbook Page

Bold color, depth and dimension enhance this page.

SIZE: 12" x 12"

MATERIALS:
Felt (Red, White, Blue) • 12" x 12" Tar cardstock • White chipboard letters • Embroidery floss (White, Red) • Buttons • Silver brads • Black marker • Adhesive

INSTRUCTIONS:
1. Cut out felt stars and letters.
2. Whipstitch around Red star and entire edge of Tan cardstock with White floss.
3. Sew buttons to White star with Rec floss.
4. Add Silver brads to Blue star.
5. Adhere photo to back of page. Dra a dash and dot line around the photo
6. Adhere stars and letters to page.

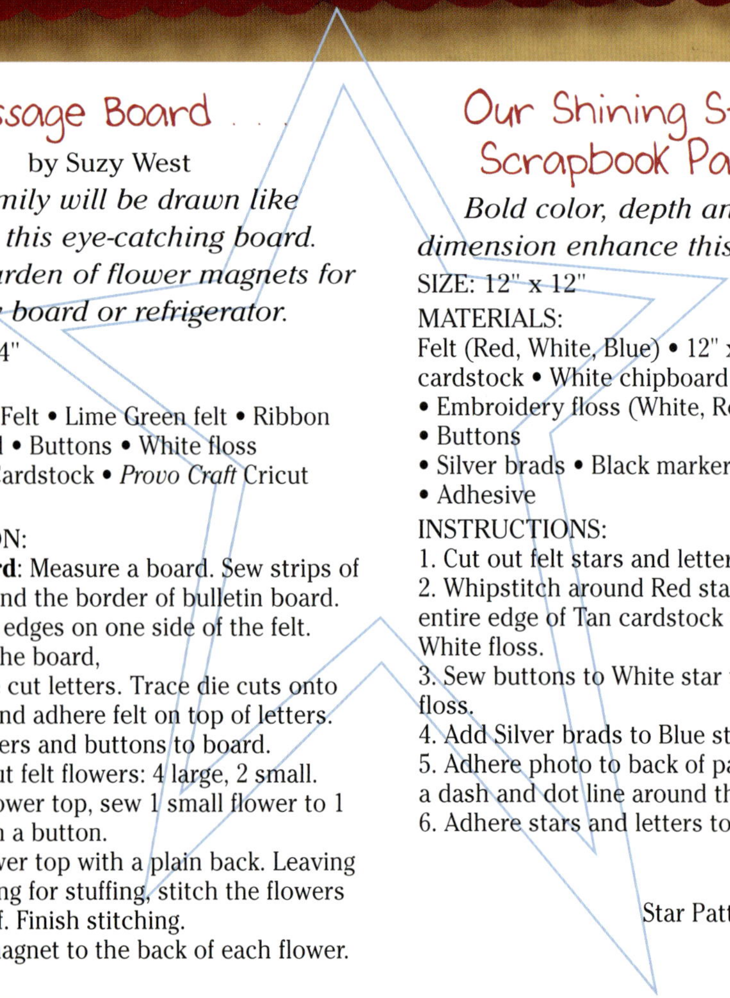

Star Patterns

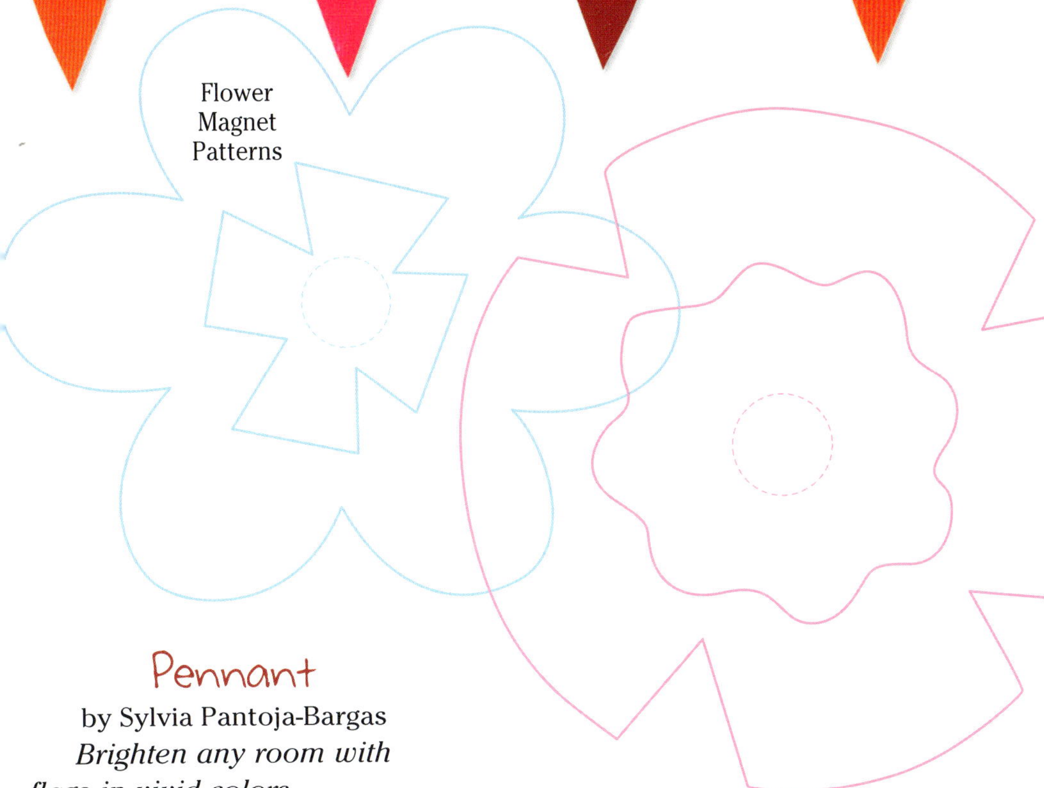

Flower Magnet Patterns

Invitation

Get the attention your announcement deserves. This invitation will not be overlooked in the mail.

SIZE: 3¾" x 8½"

MATERIALS:
Felt (Hot Pink, Orange) • Decorative paper • Cardstock (White, Pink, Orange) • Ball fringe • Adhesive

INSTRUCTIONS:
1. Print invitation details on White cardstock, including photo.
2. Adhere to paper, trim, set aside.
3. Cut felt and cardstock in the following colors: Pink 3¾" x 8½" for invitation, Orange 2¾" x 3¾" for pocket.
4. Adhere felt to matching cardstock.
5. Adhere pocket and ball fringe to invitation. Slide invitation details into pocket.

Pennant

by Sylvia Pantoja-Bargas

Brighten any room with flags in vivid colors.

SIZE: 6½" x 60"

MATERIALS:
8" x 8" Felt (Red, Pink, Orange) • 60" Red ribbon • 20" each Orange and Hot Pink ball fringe • Adhesive

INSTRUCTIONS:
1. Cut 2 triangles from each color of felt (5" wide x 6½" high)
2. Adhere to Red ribbon
3. Add ball fringe.

Purse Party Favor

Thank your guests for coming to the party with a fashionable and fun felt purse.

SIZE: 7" x 8½"

MATERIALS:
Felt (Red, Hot Pink, Orange) • Ribbon (2 strips 9" Red grosgrain ribbon ⅝" wide; 6" Orange ¼" wide for • 6" each ball fringe (Orange, Hot Pink) • Cardstock (Red 1¼" x 2½", White 1" x 2¼") • Adhesive

INSTRUCTIONS:
1. Cut Red felt in shape of a purse.
2. Glue ribbon handles to purse.
3. Add felt strips and ball fringe to front of purse.
4. Tape White cardstock to Red cardstock. Write 'Thank You' message. Punch a hole in the corner and tie to purse with Orange ribbon.

Pom Poms

Here is a fun and easy way to make dimensional accents for frames, pillows, book covers, decor... well almost anything.

1. Wrap yarn around a Pom Pom tool.

2. Close the tool, then tie yarn around the center.

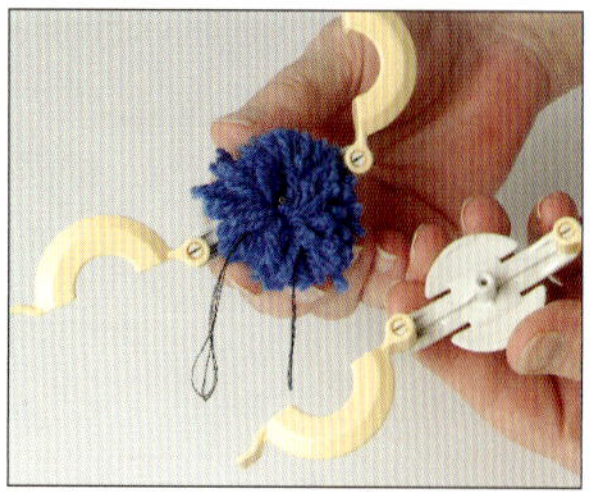

3. Clip yarn, then remove from the tool.

Thank You Canister

by Nichole Pereira

Say "thank you" to someone thoughtful with this pretty container. Fill it with yummy treats.

SIZE: 1¾" diameter, 5" tall

MATERIALS:

Turquoise felt • Decorative paper • Canister • Ribbon • 'thank you' tag • Red cardstock • Button • Embroidery floss (Yellow, Orange) • Sewing machine • Thread • Craft glue

INSTRUCTIONS:

1. Cut cardstock to cover about ⅔ of the lower portion of the canister. Cut felt the same size.
2. Stitch designs on the felt using embroidery floss.
3. Sew the felt to the cardstock and glue to the canister.
4. Cut decorative paper to cover the remainder of canister.
5. Use ribbon to cover the seam, and attach tag.
6. Trace the top onto cardstock and felt. Cut out.
7. Sew felt to cardstock. Sew a button in place. Adhere to the top.

Sketchbook

by Nichole Pereira

Record your sketches, project ideas, and creative notes in this fun book.

SIZE: 5" x 8"

MATERIALS:

Felt • Sketchbook • Decorative paper • Scalloped paper • Red pearl cotton • Ribbon • Rub-ons • Rhinestones • Buttons • Magnetic closure

INSTRUCTIONS:

1. **Book**: Cover the front and back of the sketchbook with decorative papers.
2. Cover the seam with ribbon. Apply rub-ons for the word "sketches".
3. Cover the spine with felt. Add the rhinestones.
4. Adhere the scalloped paper to the left edge and cut any excess.
5. **Flower**: Cut 3 felt circles: 2½", 2" 1¾". Whipstitch around the edges with pearl cotton and use a button for the center of the flower.
6. **Closure**: Cut a small strip of felt and adhere it to the back of the sketchbook so that half of it hangs off the edge. Adhere the flower to the front of the strip.
7. Add magnet underneath flower and on top of book.

Princess Pillow

Sylvia Pantoja-Bargas

Display your child's name on a colorful decorative pillow.

SIZE: 9½" x 9½"

MATERIALS:

Felt (Turquoise, Red) • White felt letters • Red rickrack • Red floss • Crown jewels • Polyfil stuffing • Felt glue

INSTRUCTIONS:

1. Cut 2 Turquoise felt squares 9" x 9".
2. Adhere all 4 sides with felt glue with opening for stuffing.
3. Stuff with polyfil, sew opening with Red floss.
4. Glue Red heart, White letters, crown jewel, and rickrack in place.

Friendsship Mini Book

by Sylvia Pantoja-Bargas

Create your own little book of memories to treasure forever.

SIZE: 3¼" x 7¼"

MATERIALS:

Turquoise felt • Red felt flowers • White chipboard letters • Lined paper • Rub-ons • White cardstock • Chipboard • Ribbon • Brads • Binder rings

Mini Book Pattern

INSTRUCTIONS:

1. Cut felt, 4 inside pages, and chipboard back cover 3¼" x 7¼".
2. Decorate pages and cover.
3. Punch 2 holes through all pages, and covers.
4. Add binder rings and ribbons.

Fronts and Backs of Coasters

Family Coasters

by Rocio Duran

If it doesn't move, embellish it! Even corkboard coasters can be covered with felt and decorated - just for fun. Now everyone in the family can have their own individual coaster.

SIZE: 4" x 5"

MATERIALS:

Felt (Blue, Red, Tan, Yellow) • White Stiffened Eazy Felt • Cork • Chipboard • Flowers • 4 yds of ribbon • Clear rhinestones • Tags • Brads • Chipboard Crown and letters • Buttons • Brown Scribbles 3D paint • *McGill* Round Tab punch • Embroidery floss (Tan, Red, Green) • Decorative paper • Cardstock • Crop-A-Dile • Adhesive

INSTRUCTIONS:

1. **Coasters**: Cut stiffened felt, chipboard and cork 4" x 5".
2. Decorate felt and cork.
3. Add a round tab punch to each felt piece.
4. With a Crop-A-Dile, punch holes around each felt, chipboard and cork.
5. Thread ribbon thru all the holes. Add tag and tie ribbon.
6. Glue together felt, chipboard and cork.
7. **Box**: Using a large piece of stiffened felt, fold on 3 sides enough to cover all coasters.
8. At the corners fold excess inward and Whipstitch around the edges of the box.
9. Decorate outside of box.

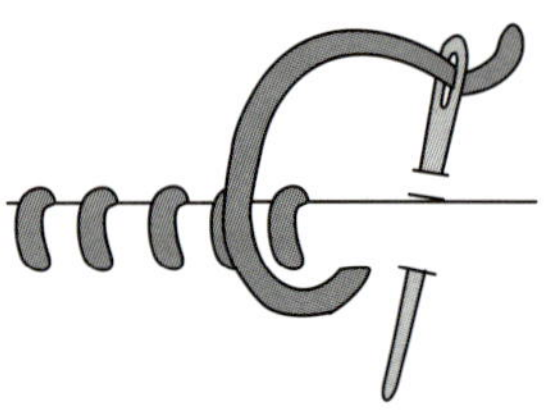

Whip Stitch

Insert a needle under the bottom layer of fabric. Bring needle up through the top layer of fabric. Use this stitch around edges.

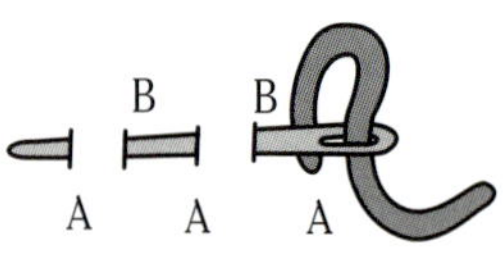

Running Stitch

Come up at A. Weave a needle through fabric. Make short, even stitches. Use this stitch for edges or to gather fabric.

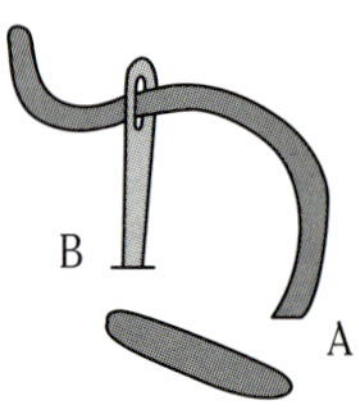

Straight Stitch

Come up at A and go down at B to form a simple flat stitch. Use this stitch for hair for animals and for simple petals on small flowers.

Felt Picture Frame

by Nichole Pereira

Dig into your button stash to create a frame.

SIZE: 8" x 8" MATERIALS:
Brown felt • 8" x 8" frame with 3" x 3" window • Cardstock • Buttons • Brown embroidery floss • Sticker • Red ribbon • Red acrylic paint • Sewing machine • Thread • Craft glue

INSTRUCTIONS:
1. Paint the frame Red. Let dry.
2. Trace the frame onto cardstock. Cut out cardstock and felt.
3. Zigzag stitch felt to the cardstock.
4. Sew buttons with embroidery floss.
5. Tie the tag around the edge and adhere to the frame.

Flower Frames

Pretty border stitching adds a designer touch to these felt-covered frames.

SIZE: 4" diameter

MATERIALS:
Felt (Pink, Brown) • 3 flower frames 4" diameter • Embroidery floss (Pink, Brown) • Buttons • Adhesive

INSTRUCTIONS:
1. Trace each frame onto felt and cut out.
2. Whipstitch around the edge of each felt flower.
3. Embroider flowers and sew buttons as desired.
4. Adhere felt to each frame.

Lampshade Pattern

Felt Frame

by Suzy West

It's so easy to cover a frame with felt. Hand stitches and a flower make the project uniquely yours.

SIZE: 5" x 7"

MATERIALS: Felt (White, Pink, Blue, Green) • 5" x 7" frame • Buttons • Green floss
• Blue rickrack • Adhesive

INSTRUCTIONS:
1. Trace frame onto felt and cut out.
2. Stitch the pieces together and adhere to the frame.
3. Cut out the flower pieces and leaves.
4. Attach flower petals with button. Adhere flower, rickrack, and leaf to the frame.

Pretty Lampshade

Light up your life and your room with a pretty lampshade covered in felt with your favorite embellishments.

SIZE: 9" tall, 11" diameter

MATERIALS:
Felt (Pink, White, Blue, Green) • Lamp shade • Brads • Buttons • Embroidery floss (Blue, Green) • Adhesive

INSTRUCTIONS:
1. Trace lampshade onto paper to make a pattern.
2. Cut felt pieces to fit the pattern.
3. Stitch felt pieces together.
4. Cut out hearts, butterfly, and flower parts. Add buttons, brads, and floss to the shapes. Adhere pieces to felt.
5. Add buttons on the White pieces of felt.
6. Adhere the felt to the lampshade.

'Ten Things I Love' Mini-Book

by Rocio Duran

Create a unique biography with images and words that tell of your passions, favorite things, and the people you love.

SIZE: 4" x 4" x 1½" deep

MATERIALS:

Stiffened Eazy Felt (Green, Black) • Wood box • Ribbons • Flowers • Rub-ons • Rhinestones • Chipboard letters • Eyelets • Brads • Decorative paper • Cardstock • *7gypsies* round stamp • Crop-A-Dile • White Scribbles 3D paint • Pink acrylic paint • Paintbrush • Eyelet tools • Adhesive

INSTRUCTIONS:

1. **Box**: Paint wood box Pink. Let it dry.
2. Adhere decorative paper on sides and bottom of box.
3. Add title to top lid of the box. Add 3D paint dots to the title.
4. Cut the Green felt in a rickrack pattern and glue around lid. Add rhinestones.
5. **Accordion pages**: Cut 6 stiffened felt pieces to fit inside box.
6. Punch 3 holes to left and right side of 4 felt pieces. For the other 2 felt pieces only punch holes on 1 side only.
7. Set eyelets in each hole.
8. Tie each piece of felt together with ribbon to make an accordion mini-book.
9. Adhere the back page to the inside of the box.
10. Decorate pages as desired.